THE STORY OF SOLAR ENERGY

Arvind Gupta

Illustrated by Reshma Barve

SCHOLASTIC
New York Toronto London Auckland
Sydney New Delhi Hong Kong

ARVIND GUPTA graduated from the Indian Institute of Technology, Kanpur (1975) with a degree in Electrical Engineering. He has written 15 books on science activities, translated 140 books into Hindi and presented 125 films on science activities on *Doordarshan*. His first book *Matchstick Models & Other Science Experiments* was translated into 12 Indian languages and sold over half a million copies. He has received several honours, including the inaugural *National Award for Science Popularization amongst Children* (1988), *Distinguished Alumnus Award of IIT, Kanpur* (2000), *Indira Gandhi Award for Science Popularization* (2008) and the *Third World Academy of Science Award* (2010) for making science interesting for children.
Currently he works at IUCAA's Children's Science Center, Pune, and shares his passion for books and toys through his website http://arvindguptatoys.com

RESHMA BARVE studied Commercial Arts at the Abhinav Kala Mahavidyalaya, Pune. She is a freelance artist and designer and has illustrated many children's books.

Published by Scholastic India Pvt. Ltd.
A subsidiary of Scholastic Inc., New York, 10012 (USA).
Publishers since 1920, with international operations in Canada,
Australia, New Zealand, the United Kingdom, India, and Hong Kong.

For information regarding permission, write to:
Scholastic India Pvt. Ltd.
Golf View Corporate Tower-A, 3rd Floor,
DLF Phase V, Gurgaon 122002 (India)

First edition: December 2011
This reprint edition: October 2023

ISBN-13: 978-81-8477-828-1

Printed in India at Shivam Offset Press, New Delhi

New Clear Energy

The sun is everywhere. In India we see too much of it. But instead of sweating in it, we can try and make the sun do useful work like cooking food and lighting homes. On a sunny day, the sun's energy falling on an area of 150 cm^2 exceeds the energy released by the kitchen gas stove at full throttle! If we just collect that energy and concentrate it at one spot we'll be able to cook without any fuel!

We are blessed with abundant sunshine, a good enough reason to seriously engage with this perpetual, non-polluting energy source. But enough research has not been done on solar energy. In a country where 400 million people live without electricity, we need to figure out a way to design cheap solar cells and to make efficient solar cookers. Solar energy holds the potential to provide even the remotest Indian hut with electricity.

India has made a good beginning with wind energy. One private company alone has installed over 6000 megawatts of non-polluting wind power. This story needs to be repeated with solar energy.

ACKNOWLEDGEMENTS

Several sterling individuals helped me with this book. Dr Anirban Hazra and Anish Mokashi sent me many books for research. Priya Kamath's initial drawings paved the way for the book. Whenever the 'sun' book came under a 'cloud' my colleague Dr Vidula Mhaiskar found me unexpected shafts of 'sunshine' to brighten it.

Thanks to my journalist friend Neela Sharma for discovering the young illustrator and designer Reshma Barve. Her deep sensitivity has imbued this book with life. I hope children and adults alike will enjoy this comic book and that it will bring a little sunshine into their lives.

I would specially like to thank Dr Arnab Bhattacharya, Dr T. Sampath Kumar, Alabhya Singh, Joyce, Nyla Coelho, Pavan Iyengar, Rajkishore and many other dear friends for critically reviewing the manuscript and suggesting changes.

Finally, I would like to thank the Inter-University Centre for Astronomy & Astrophysics for nurturing this project, and the Navajibai Ratan Tata Trust for providing the financial support for preparing this manuscript.

Arvind Gupta

BIG BANG
It all started with the BIG BANG.
Our earth is 4.6 billion years old.
The first fuel used on earth was wood. But when forests became scarce people burnt coal.
Soon the coal on the surface got used up. So miners dug deeper. And then the deep mines became waterlogged.
Watt's that?
Samuel Newcombe invented a steam engine that could pump out water from deep mines.
James Watt designed the first practical steam engine in 1769.

COAL MINE
Cheap coal and the steam engine powered the economy and ushered the Industrial Revolution in to England.
Rails made it easier to haul coal from one place to another.
Michael Faraday invented the first Electric Motor.
Nicola Tesla invented Alternating Current (AC).
Coal miners have to dig deeper and deeper and deeper
Coal was burnt to generate steam. Steam turned electric turbines.
Edwin Drake built the first rock oil well in Pennsylvania.
Karl Daimler built the first automobile that ran on petrol.
The Wright Brothers started fuel aviation.

Coal tar and oil were used to make industrial chemicals. Modern medicines use these chemicals to cure diseases and prolong life.
Industri Chemica
Medicin
Fritz Haber and Karl Bosch made fertilisers from fossil fuels like coal and oil.
fertilizer
World War I was the first major fossil fuel conflict.
Fertilisers and tractors increased food production and this helped in feeding a growing population.
World War II saw the use of guided missiles and atom bombs.
After World War II was over, large manufacturing capacities were set up as an optimistic reaction to the devastation the war had caused.

Assembly lines made goods faster than people needed them.
Advertisers used the television to hook new consumers.
The demand for energy soared.
Soon there was an energy crisis. Oil prices ZOOMED. In the 1970s the Arab countries nationalised their oil industry. People were shocked to find out how dependent economies were on oil.
The energy crisis gave birth to the environmental movement. Rachel Carson's classic book SILENT SPRING shows how pesticides poison the earth.
But when oil prices fell everyone forgot about the energy shortage.
There was a showdown between the market and planned economy. Markets won all the way. The Soviet Union collapsed in 1991.
Personal computers became common.
Globalisation arrived. Cheap labour in China produced all kinds of things for the world.
Soon there was a cell phone in almost every hand.

Today world oil production has dipped. China now burns a large portion of the world's remaining coal to make exports possible. But where will it get more coal and oil to fuel more growth?
COAL
Environmental problems are everywhere.
Rising CO_2 levels have led to record heat waves.
There have been massive floods and droughts. Top soil has been eroding into the sea.
Ice caps have started to melt because of global warming.
Mount Everest
Ancient forests have disappeared. Species have gone extinct at a 1000 times the normal rate of extinction.
Fresh water has been polluted by industrial wastes.
To increase yields oil companies have drilled miles deep in the sea. But in the Gulf of Mexico an oil platform EXPLODED in 2010 ...
... and fouled up the sea.

The West reinvented itself as a KNOWLEDGE economy.
Jobs were outsourced to developing nations, poorer countries became the dumping ground for e-waste.
40% of the economy was dependent on the finance sector.
CASINO
In 2007, the biggest slump since the 1930s broke out. Five years later we're still suffering its repercussions. Unemployment soared. Credit evaporated. The economy was on the verge of a collapse.
No Vacancy
It's amazing how far we have come since the beginning of industrialisation 200 years ago. But this reckless pace of growth and consumerist lifestyle cannot be sustained for long.
Where are we headed? What does the future hold for us?
Can we keep increasing our population exponentially? Can we keep ravaging the earth?
Can we keep releasing more carbon into the atmosphere?
Can we continue poisoning the earth with more chemicals and pesticides?

The US fritters away billions of dollars a day fighting wars in Iraq and Afghanistan leading to a serious debt crisis. It has been on an exhilarating consumerist ride, but is now faced with its limits.
We have to learn from past mistakes.
We need to learn to live without fossil fuels while supporting the livelihood of 7 billion people at a sustainable level.
LUMBER
We have to deal with our legacy of environmental destruction.
In other words, we have to live within nature's budget of renewable resources and keep in mind the rate of natural replenishment.
Alternative energy sources are important but it will be very difficult to fully replace coal, oil and gas in the near future ...

We speak of
'producing' oil
as if it were
made in
a factory.
But only
nature produces oil.
And all we do
is mine and
burn it up.

We must turn
to the SUN
and seek elegant ways
to live within
the renewable
energy income
it bestows
upon us.

Life on earth evolved and was nurtured by the sun. The sun keeps delivering large amounts of energy to the earth each second.

The sun will keep doing this for the next 5 billion years.

Plants bend to catch the sun and produce all their food using sunshine.

Kings of yore pegged their lineage to the sun. Some called themselves Suryavanshis, descendants of the sun.

The 13th century Konark temple in Odisha, India is dedicated to the sun god SURYA.

The poet Rabindranath Tagore wrote of Konark:

'Here the language of stone surpasses the language of man.'

This chariot-shaped stone temple has twelve pairs of exquisitely decorated wheels drawn by seven spirited horses. The temple symbolises the majestic stride of the sun god.

THE SUN IN DIFFERENT CULTURES

RA was the most important god of the Egyptians. He was considered the lord of all gods and was depicted in human form with a falcon head, crowned with the sun disc encircled by a sacred cobra.

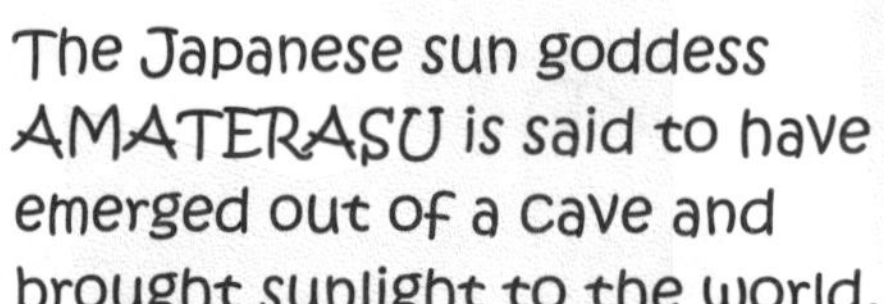

The Japanese sun goddess AMATERASU is said to have emerged out of a cave and brought sunlight to the world.

HOW TO REACH THE SUN ON A PIECE OF PAPER

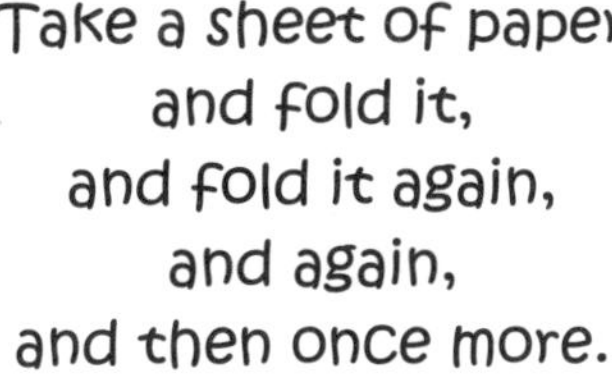

Take a sheet of paper
and fold it,
and fold it again,
and again,
and then once more.

By the 6th fold it will
be 1-centimetre thick.
By the 11th fold it will be
32-centimetre thick,
and by the 15th fold 5 metres.
At the 20th fold it will measure 160 metres.
At the 24th fold 2.5 kilometres,
and by fold 30 it will be 160 kilometres high.
At the 35th fold it will be 5000 kilometres.
At the 43rd fold it will reach the moon.
And by fold 52
it will stretch from here to the sun!

If the earth kept absorbing the sun's energy day after day, it would become boiling hot. Fortunately, the earth gets rid of the energy it gains during the day at night. This balance between energy coming by day and going by night keeps the temperature just right on our planet.

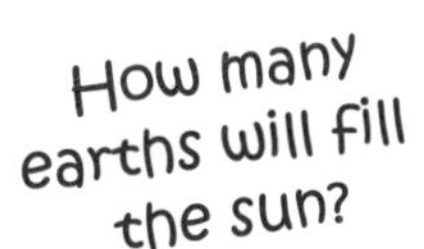

The sun is 400 times wider than the moon. Then why do they look the same size from the earth?

Because the sun is 400 times farther from the earth than the moon.

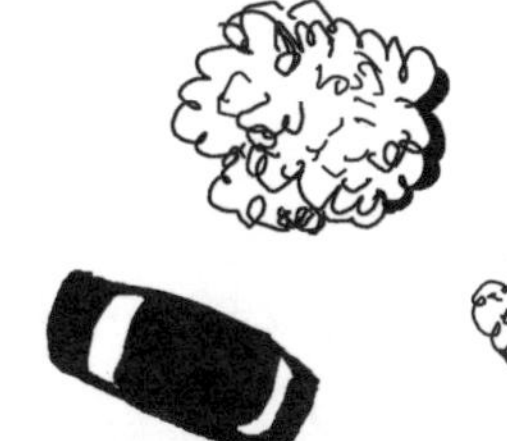

GREEK FREAK

Socrates said, 'An ideal house should be cool in summer and warm in winter.' But this was not easy to accomplish 2500 years ago. The Greeks had no artificial means of cooling their homes during summer or heating them during winter.

Forests in Greece were ravaged for wood which was needed for cooking and heating. Trees were also required to build homes and ships. By the 5th century BC Greece was completely denuded of trees. When wood became scarce the search for alternatives began.

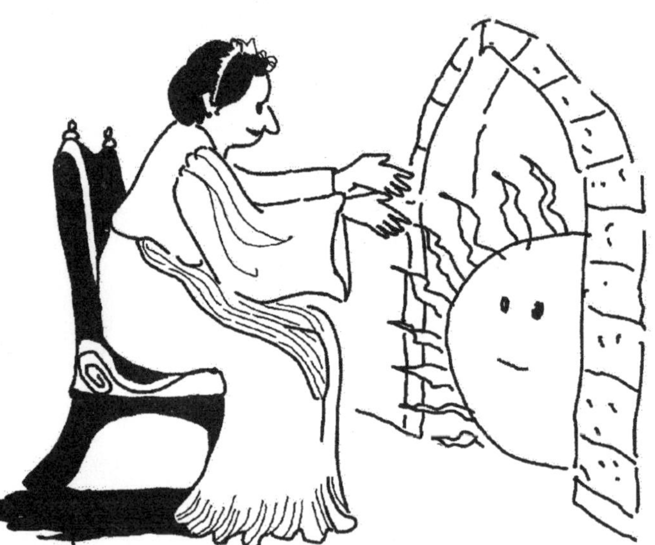

Fortunately, the sun was free and plentiful. The Greeks learnt to warm their houses with the winter sun and avoided it during the summers. The Greeks were pioneering SOLAR ARCHITECTS.

The Greeks knew that the sun was low in the sky during the winters and overhead during the summers.

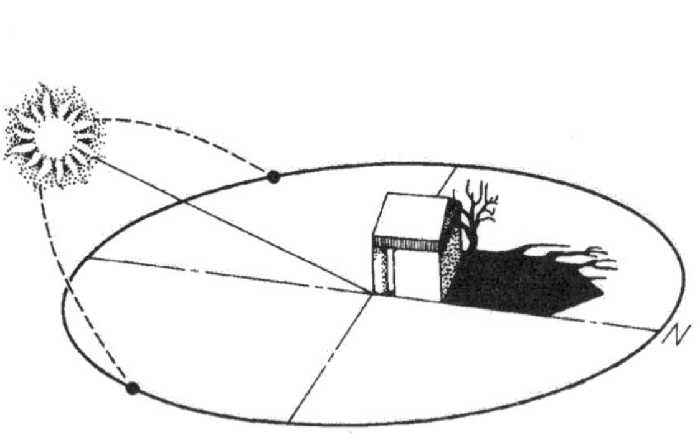

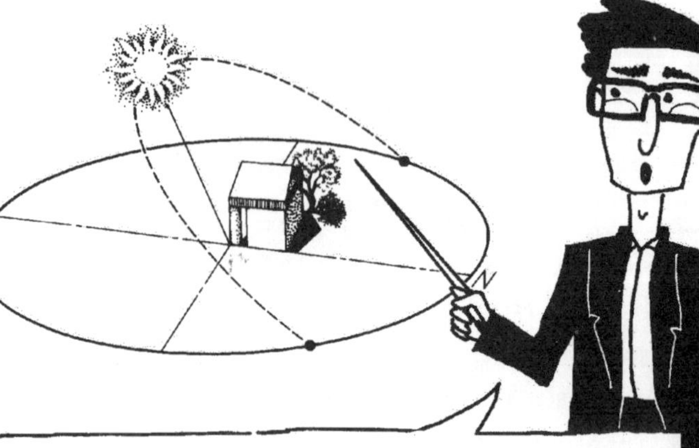

So they built their houses in such a way that the winter sunlight entered and warmed them. With eaves and overhanging roofs they kept their houses cool during summers.

GLASS CLASS

The Romans consumed even more wood than the Greeks. Wood was in heavy demand for building houses and ships, and for heating public baths and private villas.
Once the Romans ran out of wood they had no choice but to learn from the Greeks. The Romans didn't just copy the Greeks. They did even better and advanced solar technology.

In the 1st century AD the Romans used transparent materials like mica to make WINDOWS. This let the sunlight in but kept out the rain, snow and cold.

They also oriented their houses so that they could catch the sun.

The Romans were the first to use GLASS to enhance solar heating. The sunlight got in through the glass and warmed the house in winter. The warm air couldn't get out and stayed in, raising the temperature inside the house.

The Romans also built GREENHOUSES and public baths. They were the first to enact SUN RIGHTS in their laws.

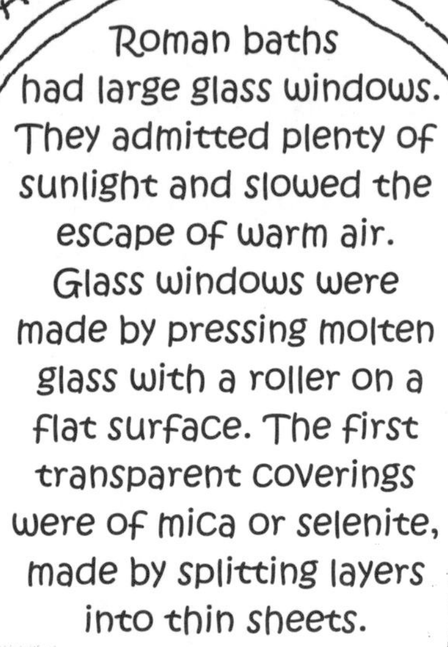

The Roman emperor Tiberius loved cucumbers and wanted them the whole year round. The gardeners thought of a great idea. They mounted cucumber beds on trolleys which could be wheeled into the sun. In winter they covered them with transparent material to hold the solar heat.

The Romans venerated the sun.
Doctors considered the sun good for many ailments.

Can the sun's rays be concentrated into a small area? More energy would thus pour into this small area raising its temperature. The Greeks discovered that light reflecting from a curved polished metal that is concave (KON-kave = curved inwards) can concentrate the sun's rays at a point.

This can be understood through a simple experiment. Fix 3 pencils into an old rubber slipper. The pencils at right angles represent parallel rays striking a plane mirror. On bending the slipper inwards the pencils will meet at a point called the FOCUS.

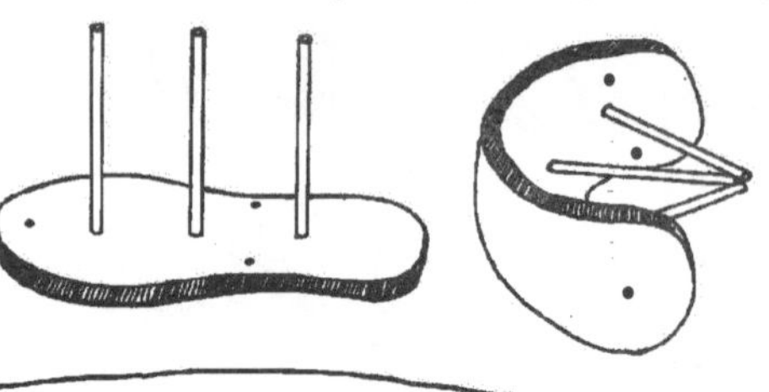

(FOH-kus) means FIREPLACE in Latin.

BURNING MIRRORS

The Greeks made the first 'burning mirrors' out of polished metal. These curved mirrors could collect and concentrate the sun's rays on to an object with enough intensity to make it burst into flames within seconds.

Initially the curved mirrors used were half-spheres. But they did not concentrate rays to a point. In 230 BC, the Greek mathematician Dositheus showed that a parabolic mirror worked better.

doh-SITH-eeoos

A PARABOLIC mirror is not a half-sphere but more like the small end of a half-egg.

The word LENS comes from its shape which is like a half LENtil (pulse).

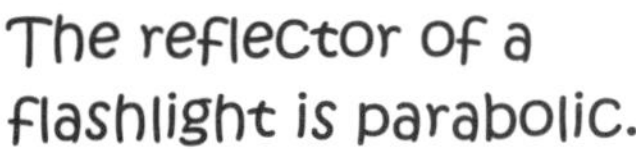

The reflector of a flashlight is parabolic.

According to a story the Greek mathematician Archimedes built pretty good mirrors. In 214 BC, when the Romans besieged the city of Syracuse on the coast of Sicily, Archimedes supposedly used mirrors to reflect sunlight towards the enemy ships and set them on fire.

Al-Haitham's Opticae Thesaurus

Burning mirrors were not really used in war, instead they were used to ignite CEREMONIAL FIRES in temples of worship. Sun fire was thought to be UNPOLLUTED, PURE AND HOLY.

FUN WITH A BURNING MIRROR

Warning: Don't try this on your skin or eyes

Hang a nail by a black thread in a bottle. You can concentrate rays from the outside with a magnifying glass and burn the thread. It won't work with a white thread.

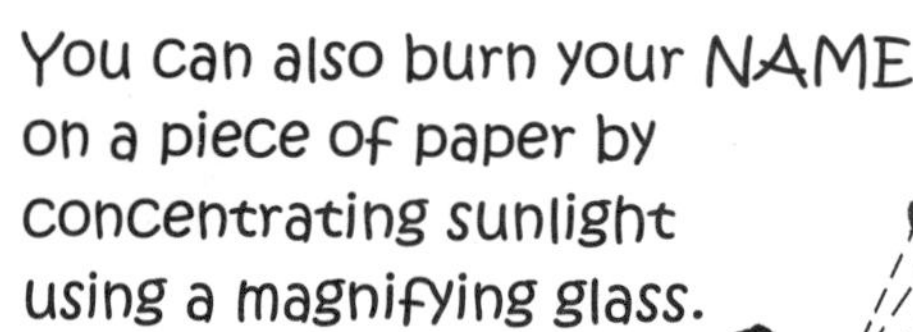

You can also burn your NAME on a piece of paper by concentrating sunlight using a magnifying glass.

During the Dark Ages of Europe, scholarship flourished in the Arab world. Al-Haitham, an 11th century Arabic scholar based in Cairo experimented and wrote at length about BURNING MIRRORS.

In the 13th century, Roger Bacon, a Christian monk read Al-Haitham's essays.

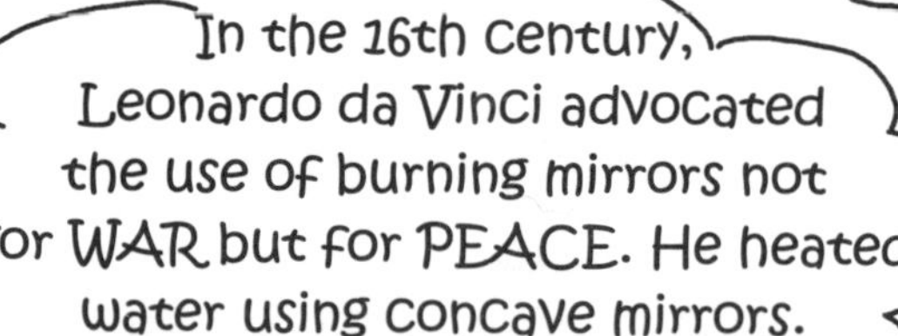

He wanted to make weapons using burning mirrors. In those days the Church engaged heavily in metaphysical speculation. It debated issues of hell, heaven and the soul. So a weapon was a leap forward from speculative theology. It meant engaging with the real world, doing real experiments.

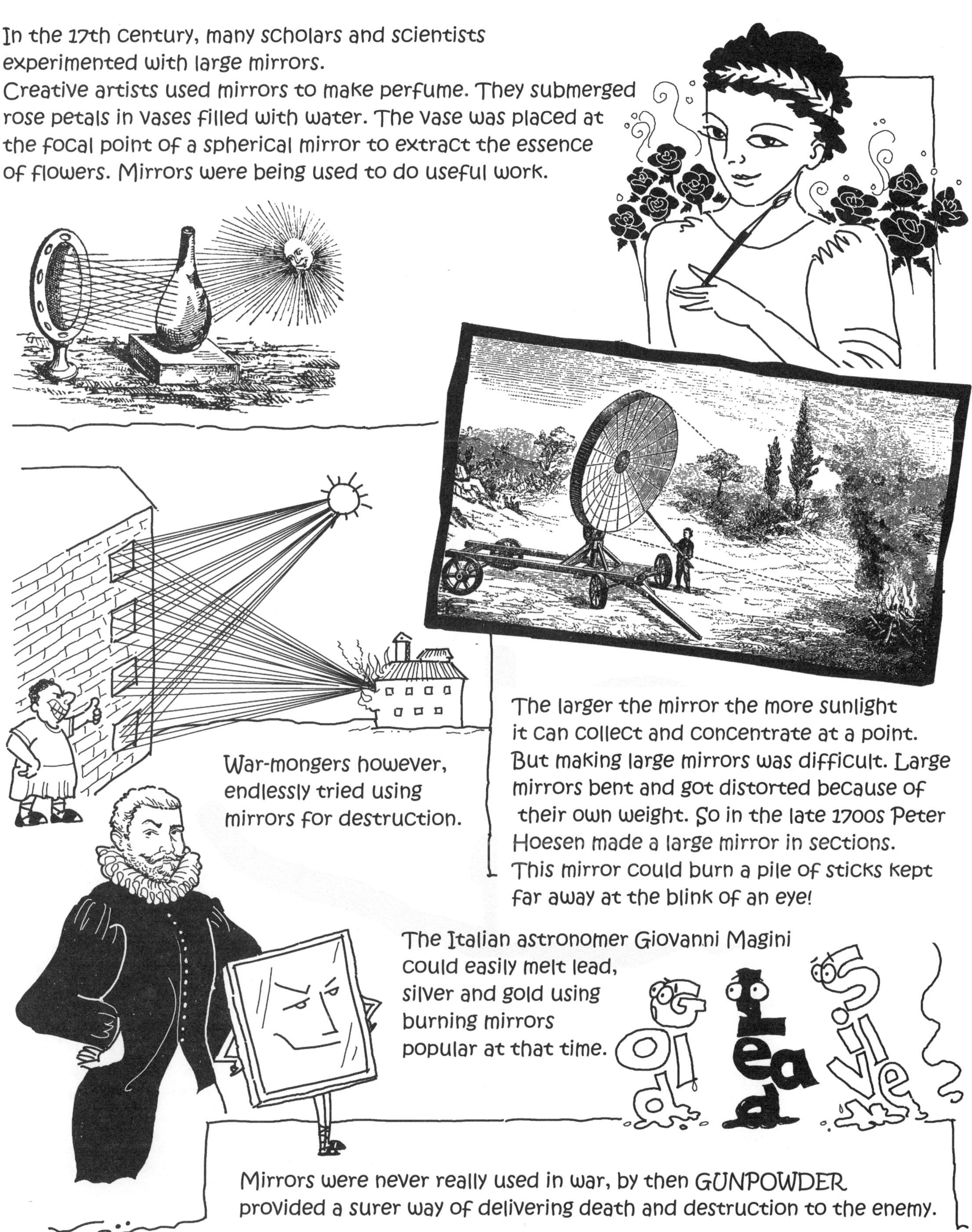
In the 17th century, many scholars and scientists experimented with large mirrors.
Creative artists used mirrors to make perfume. They submerged rose petals in vases filled with water. The vase was placed at the focal point of a spherical mirror to extract the essence of flowers. Mirrors were being used to do useful work.
War-mongers however, endlessly tried using mirrors for destruction.
The larger the mirror the more sunlight it can collect and concentrate at a point. But making large mirrors was difficult. Large mirrors bent and got distorted because of their own weight. So in the late 1700s Peter Hoesen made a large mirror in sections. This mirror could burn a pile of sticks kept far away at the blink of an eye!
The Italian astronomer Giovanni Magini could easily melt lead, silver and gold using burning mirrors popular at that time.
Mirrors were never really used in war, by then GUNPOWDER provided a surer way of delivering death and destruction to the enemy.

The Orthodox Church always opposed experimentation. They were forever speculating and debating metaphysical questions like, 'How many fairies can dance on a pin head?'

A hardworking priest who tried to grow fruits to nurture the 'body' instead of the 'soul' was burnt at the stake for practising witchcraft. But science eventually broke religious dogma.

GREENHOUSES

In the inhospitable winters of Europe people started growing fruits and vegetables in greenhouses. They grew plants on inclined roofs. These south-facing slanted walls collected more sunlight. Plants grew better on these sloping walls.

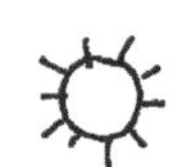

The 18th century became the AGE OF THE GREENHOUSE.

Soon the Dutch made more efficient greenhouses, using two layers of glass with air in between acting as insulation.

However, as wealth accumulated the humble greenhouse assumed a more lavish form–the CONSERVATORY. It was not a place for growing plants, but for display, more like a drawing room to entertain guests. The Lal Bagh garden in Bangalore has a huge greenhouse.

It's a blueprint for a greenhouse.

Solar heat from the conservatory often warmed the adjoining rooms of the house.

SOLAR HOT BOXES

When the sun's rays pass through glass and enter a room, they heat it. Similarly, a car parked in the sun becomes unbearably hot because of the 'greenhouse' effect.

In 1767, a Swiss engineer Horace de Saussure (soh-SOOR) made the first solar cooker. He built a miniature greenhouse with five boxes placed one inside the other.

The innermost box became very hot. Fruits kept in it became juicy and cooked.

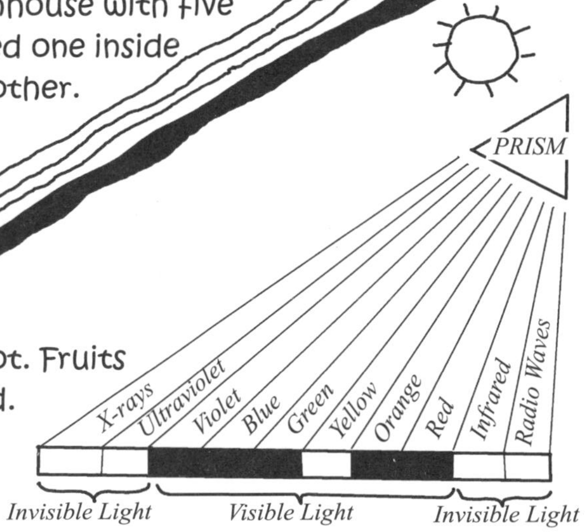

Sunshine penetrated the glass covers and was absorbed by the black surface of the boxes.

PRISM

X-rays, Ultraviolet, Violet, Blue, Green, Yellow, Orange, Red, Infrared, Radio Waves

Invisible Light — Visible Light — Invisible Light

Glass has a peculiar property. It lets in sunlight and converts it into long infrared rays. Infrared rays cannot escape the glass cover, and get trapped.

These infrared rays raise the temperature and cook food. On a clear day almost three quarters of the sun's radiation reach the earth. The earth absorbs light and releases heat.

This heat cannot readily escape the blanket of the atmosphere just like the solar heat in a 'hot box'.

Saussure tried an ambitious experiment. He measured the temperature inside his 'hot box' at two places at sea level and on top of a snow-clad mountain. At both places the temperature remained the same!

In 1830, the noted astronomer Sir John Herschel was on an expedition to the Cape of Good Hope in South Africa. In the wilderness he cooked his food on an improvised SOLAR COOKER.

He roasted eggs, cooked meat, made stew all of which were relished by entertained passers-by.

Herschel's story intrigued Samuel Langley, the American astrophysicist who later headed the Smithsonian Institute. Langley climbed Mt Whitney with his improvised 'hotbox' fitted with a thermometer to study the effect of solar energy. This is what he wrote in the 1882 issue of NATURE:

'As we slowly ascended ... and the surface temperature of the soil fell to the freezing point, the temperature in the copper vessel, over which lay two sheets of plain window glass, rose above the boiling point of water, and it was certain that we could boil water by the solar rays in such a vessel among the snow fields.'

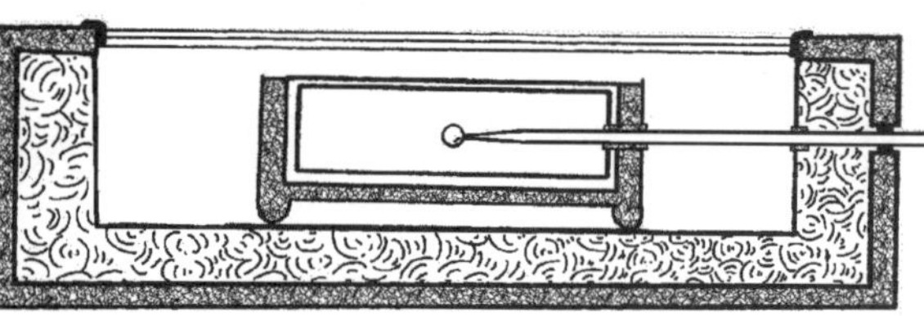

Could the energy of the sun be directly used to produce steam? One could then make a steam-powered solar engine!

In the 1st century, Hero of Alexandria built a curious solar device. He connected two containers by a tube.

When the lower container with water was placed in the sun the air inside expanded and forced the water through the tube and into the upper container doing useful work.

However, Hero's device was no more than a toy.

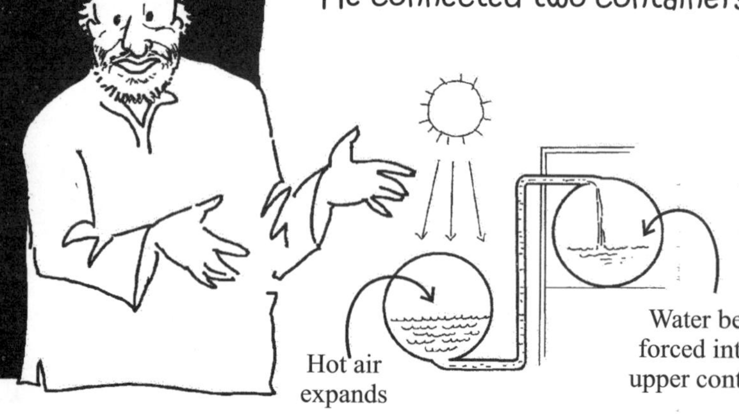

SOLAR ENGINE

With large reserves of coal, Britain became the first country to be industrialised. With no coal, France lagged behind.

In 1860, Augustine Mouchet (moo-SHOW) a French professor of mathematics made a radical suggestion that THE RAYS OF THE SUN SHOULD BE REAPED.

In 1861, Mouchet used hot boxes and made them still hotter by concentrating sunshine on them with curved mirrors.

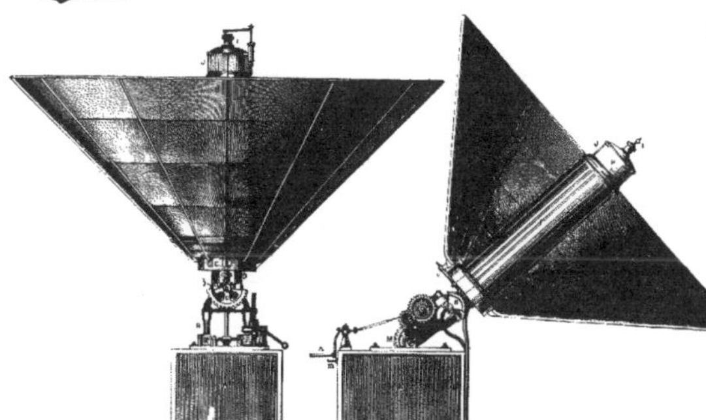

In 1866, Mouchet made the first SOLAR ENGINE. Because sunshine was not so bright in France, he moved to the French colony of Algeria.

Mouchet blackened a copper cylinder and covered it with a glass sleeve to absorb sunlight.

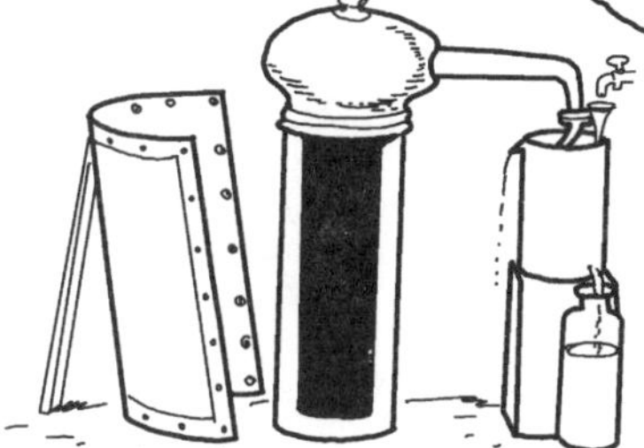

He used a parabolic mirror to concentrate sunlight from outside and successfully distilled wine using solar energy.

He baked half a kilo of bread in 45 minutes and one kilo of potatoes in an hour.

FUN WITH THE SUN

Dark surfaces absorb more heat. Place a black, a white, and a grey sheet in the sun for a while. Touch them. Which feels hotter?

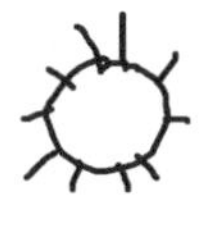

Place an ice cube each in three zip lock bags. Place them outdoors on a white, a grey and a black sheet of paper. Measure the melted water after a few minutes. Which cube melts first?

Mouchet also did preliminary investigations on the conversion of sunlight directly into electricity. However, in 1880 he returned to his university.

Mouchet's assistant Abel Pifre, took over his solar research. He built several sun motors and conducted public demonstrations to gain support for solar power.

In 1880, at the Gardens of the Tuileries in Paris, he exhibited a solar generator that drove a printing press which printed 500 copies of the Journal Soleil (SOLAR JOURNAL).

Mouchet's device, the SOLAR STILL, was widely used by settlers in Algeria to distil water laced with magnesium salts.

Mouchet's work did not usher the SUN AGE in to France but it did lay the foundation for future solar development.

In 1876, John Ericsson, a Swedish American inventor tried a very different approach.

Instead of a solar steam engine he designed a SOLAR HOT AIR ENGINE. He replaced the metallic reflector with window glass silvered on the underside.

Because the silver finish was not exposed to the elements, the mirror did not tarnish.

In 1899, Aubrey Eneas, an English inventor living in America made a solar motor using a conical reflector. In 1901, Eneas placed his solar motor on display at his friend's OSTRICH FARM.
It was an instant attention-gatherer. The handbill read:
NO EXTRA CHARGE TO SEE THE SOLAR MOTOR
The only machine of its kind in daily operation, a fifteen-horse-power engine, worked by the heat of the sun.

VISIT THE
OSTRICH FARM
100 GIGANTIC BIRDS
One of the strangest sights in the United States.—N. Y. Journal.
One of the features of Southern California.—L. A. Times.
PASADENA ELECTRIC CARS PASS THE ENTRANCE
No Extra Charge to see
THE SOLAR MOTOR
The only machine of its kind in the world in daily operation. 15-horsepower engine worked by the heat of the sun.
OPEN TO VISITORS EVERY DAY

The reflectors used by Mouchet, Ericsson and Eneas were complex and expensive. Often the moving mechanism broke down. The exposed structure was also vulnerable to high wind and weather.

There were no good tracking mechanisms at that time. So it was difficult to make the mirror face the sun all the time.

To track the sun's motion the mirror was raised and lowered by a mechanism mounted on a vertical tower behind it.

Around this time Charles Tellier (tel-YAY), a French engineer often referred to as the 'Father of Refrigeration', invented a low-temperature solar collector to drive machines. He was the first to use liquids with low boiling points for refrigeration.

Willsie and Boyle, two American engineers, furthered Tellier's ideas. They demonstrated that a solar reflector was not required to run an engine.

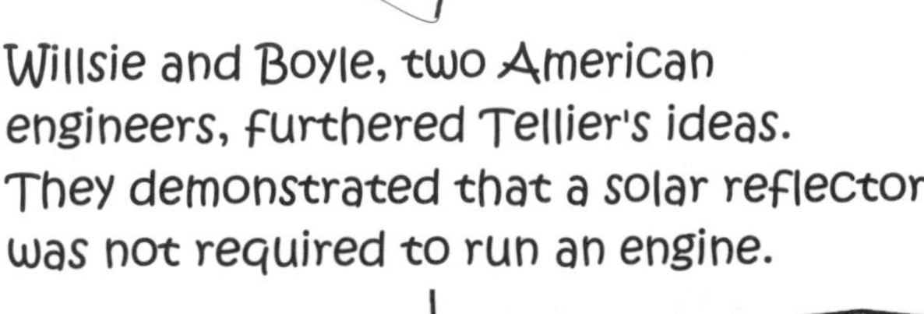

They also pointed out that a hot box could drive a low-temperature motor. They made a giant stride towards commercialising solar power.

FIRST PRACTICAL SOLAR ENGINE

In 1906, Frank Shuman, a self-taught American engineer built the first practical solar engine. He combined both hot boxes and reflectors to make solar engines more efficient. He founded the SUN POWER COMPANY and predicted, 'Ten percent of the earth's surface will eventually depend on sun power for all mechanical operations.'

Egypt, then a British colony, had plenty of sunshine. So Shuman was invited to instal a solar pump in Egypt.

The British government asked Prof C. V. Boys to review the project. Boys suggested a more efficient PARABOLIC TROUGH REFLECTOR.

Shuman's 14-HP pump could deliver 11,000 litres of water per minute, raising it 10 metres.

Stock Certificates of the Sun Power Company

111

THE SUN POWER COMPANY

This Certifies that Frank Shuman is the registered holder of Four Shares of the Capital Stock of THE SUN POWER COMPANY Transferable only on the Books of the Company by the holder hereof in person or by duly authorized Attorney upon surrender of this Certificate properly endorsed.

Witness the Seal of the Company and the signatures of its President and Treasurer this 20th day of Jany 1909

Constantine Shuman — Frank Shuman, PRESIDENT

Water need not be boiling to be useful. We only need moderately hot water to bathe. In the old days people split wood to heat water on WASH DAY. It was tough work. So they bathed only once a week.

But greater material, well-being and better personal hygiene in the 1800s increased the demand for hot water.

Soon a better way was discovered.

Metal water tanks painted black were placed tilted so that they would face the sun. They worked well. A user testified, 'Sometimes the water got so damned hot that you had to add cold water to take a bath.' But sometimes it took a very long time. What if it was a cloudy day or nighttime?

Meanwhile, Charles Haskell improved the old CLIMAX. The deep cylinder of water was replaced by a large but shallow rectangular tank. The volume of water remained the same. But now the sun's rays could penetrate deeper and heat water faster. Such water heaters worked best in warm places with a lot of sunshine like California and Florida.

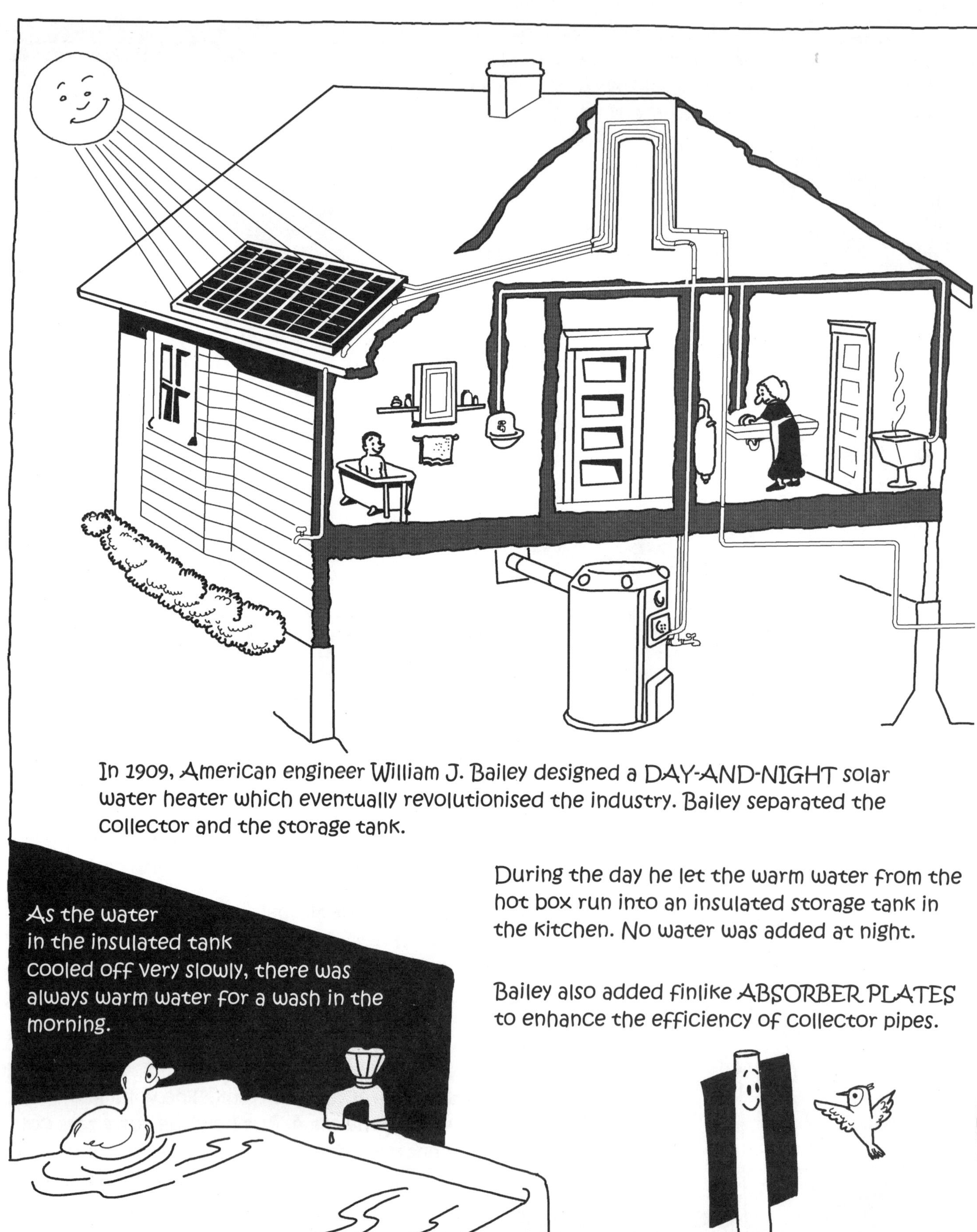
In 1909, American engineer William J. Bailey designed a DAY-AND-NIGHT solar water heater which eventually revolutionised the industry. Bailey separated the collector and the storage tank.
During the day he let the warm water from the hot box run into an insulated storage tank in the kitchen. No water was added at night.
As the water in the insulated tank cooled off very slowly, there was always warm water for a wash in the morning.
Bailey also added finlike ABSORBER PLATES to enhance the efficiency of collector pipes.

In 1913, a freak cold spell proved disastrous.
The water in the collectors froze and the copper pipes burst.
They 'popped like popcorn all over the country'.
Soon water was replaced by an anti-freeze solution.

1920 was the peak year for solar water heaters. Huge natural gas basins were discovered. Fuel prices plummetted. Gas companies offered fabulous incentives and wooed customers to use more gas.

Sales of solar water heaters slumped.

In 1931, Charles Ewald perfected a new piping pattern for the Duplex solar heater. He also used granulated cork as an insulating material between the hot-water tank and its metal shell.

SOLAR WATER HEATERS SPREAD

Then solar water heaters spread to countries which were short of fuel but had plenty of sunshine. The 1935 construction boom lifted the fortunes of the Solar Water Heater Company. Tens of thousands of new solar water heaters were installed.

Solar water heaters even travelled to Cuba with the slogan:
'WITHOUT ELECTRICITY, WITHOUT GAS, WITHOUT COAL, WITHOUT COST!'

In 1940, a young mother Rina Yissar in Israel, suffered from extreme scarcity of fuel. Most people took a cold-water bath. But Rina refused to resign to her fate. Though lacking in formal technical education, Rina had loads of common sense. She took an old tank, painted it black, filled it with water and left it out in the sun. After a few hours she had enough hot water to give her baby a warm bath.

This inspired Rina's husband Levi Yissar to harness the sun. In 1953, Levi established the Ner-Yah Company to make solar water heaters.

One of his first customers was David Ben Gurion, the founding father of Israel. He had a solar water heater installed in his house.

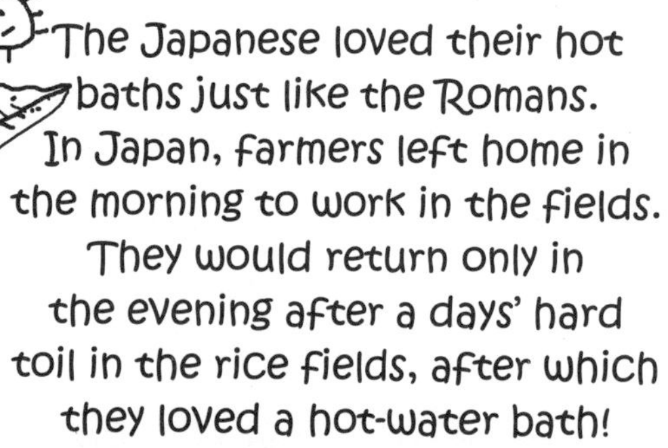

The Japanese loved their hot baths just like the Romans. In Japan, farmers left home in the morning to work in the fields. They would return only in the evening after a days' hard toil in the rice fields, after which they loved a hot-water bath!

But the traditional Japanese bathtub used large amounts of fuel.

So, during the economic depression people started using the SUN for heating water. In 1940, Sukeo Yamamoto saw farmers using an improvised solar water heater. It was a large bathtub, 2 metres long, 1 metre wide and 15 centimetres deep, filled with water. Its top was covered with a sheet of glass. Yamamoto designed the first Japanese commercial water heater. When set in the morning, the water would be sufficiently warm for a bath by afternoon.

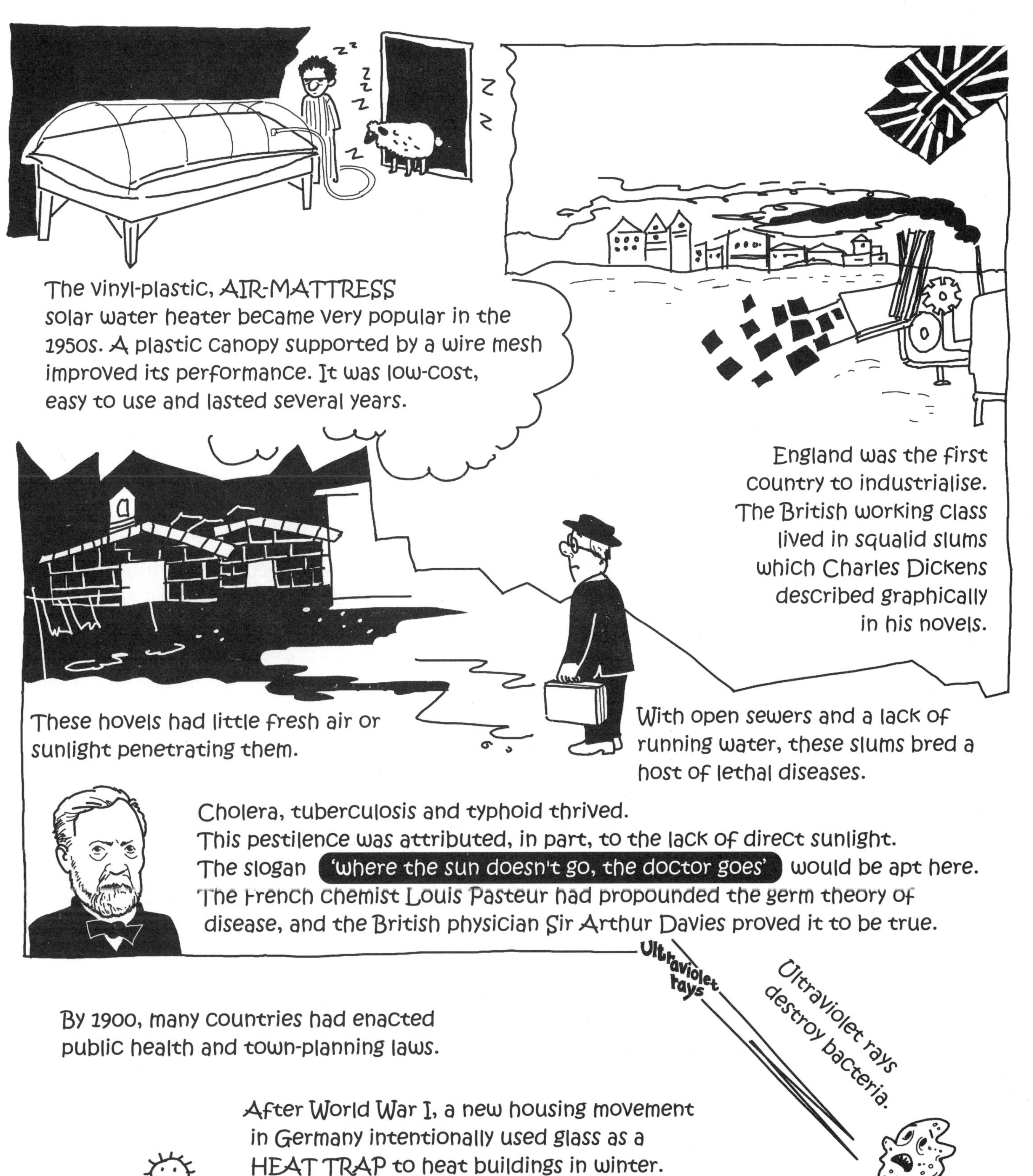

The vinyl-plastic, AIR-MATTRESS solar water heater became very popular in the 1950s. A plastic canopy supported by a wire mesh improved its performance. It was low-cost, easy to use and lasted several years.

England was the first country to industrialise. The British working class lived in squalid slums which Charles Dickens described graphically in his novels.

These hovels had little fresh air or sunlight penetrating them.

With open sewers and a lack of running water, these slums bred a host of lethal diseases.

Cholera, tuberculosis and typhoid thrived. This pestilence was attributed, in part, to the lack of direct sunlight. The slogan 'where the sun doesn't go, the doctor goes' would be apt here. The French chemist Louis Pasteur had propounded the germ theory of disease, and the British physician Sir Arthur Davies proved it to be true.

By 1900, many countries had enacted public health and town-planning laws.

After World War I, a new housing movement in Germany intentionally used glass as a HEAT TRAP to heat buildings in winter.

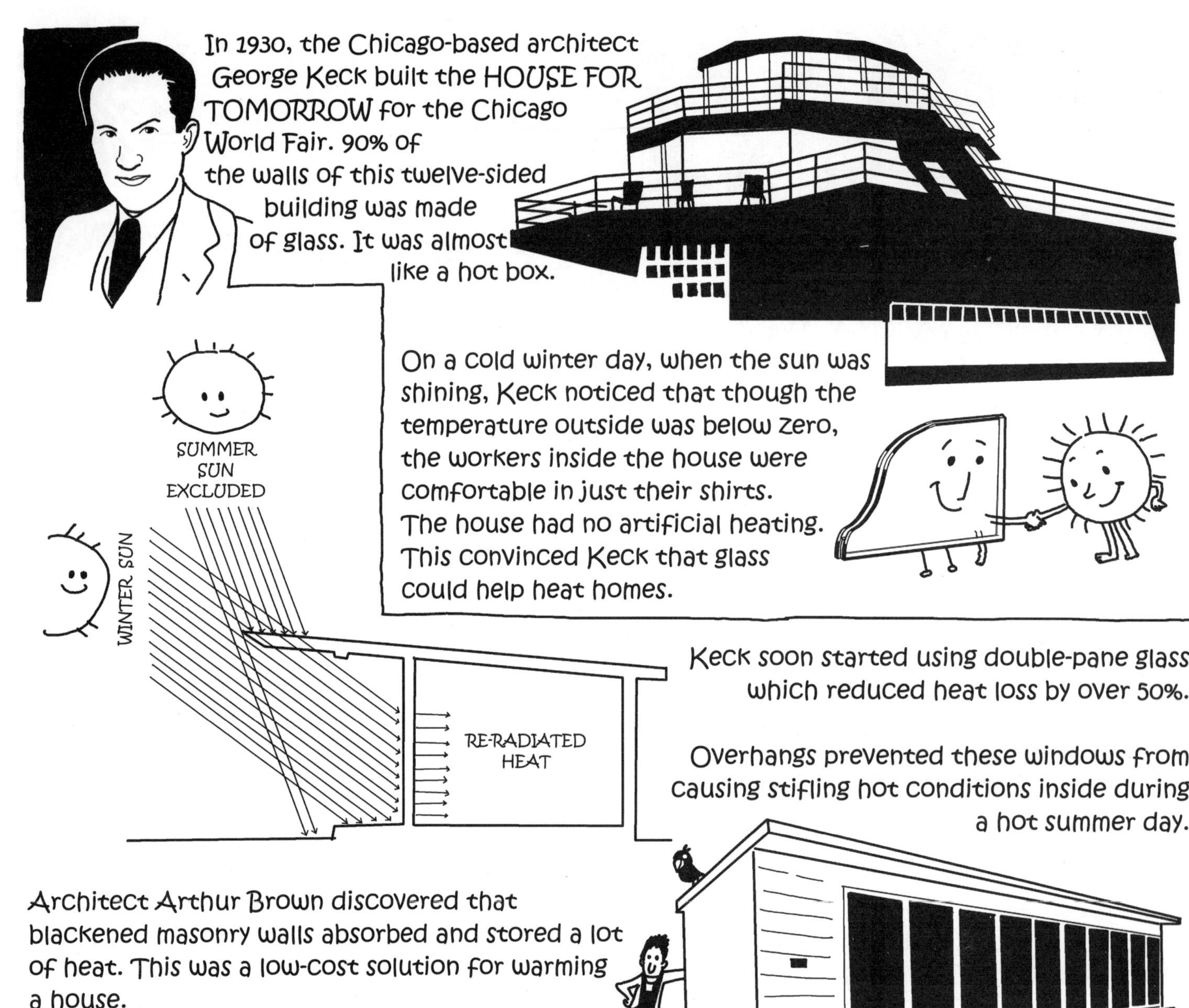

In 1930, the Chicago-based architect George Keck built the HOUSE FOR TOMORROW for the Chicago World Fair. 90% of the walls of this twelve-sided building was made of glass. It was almost like a hot box.

On a cold winter day, when the sun was shining, Keck noticed that though the temperature outside was below zero, the workers inside the house were comfortable in just their shirts. The house had no artificial heating. This convinced Keck that glass could help heat homes.

Keck soon started using double-pane glass which reduced heat loss by over 50%.

Overhangs prevented these windows from causing stifling hot conditions inside during a hot summer day.

Architect Arthur Brown discovered that blackened masonry walls absorbed and stored a lot of heat. This was a low-cost solution for warming a house.

But before long, World War II loomed on the horizon. Solar houses were 15% more expensive, so very few people wanted them.

In 1938, Hoyt Hottel at the MIT began a two-decade-long research on the use of solar collectors for heating houses. The configuration was very similar to Bailey's water heaters. Hot water from the roof ran to a storage tank below. Cool air was drawn from the rooms by fans and blown over the hot tank. The warm air was then circulated back.

In 1947, the MIT team erected a wall of water containers behind a vertical south-facing glass wall. 18-litre water cans painted black were stacked just behind the double-pane glass. Soon the water became warm and the energy was transmitted to the interior of the house. This was simpler than using flat plate collectors.

glass
water tank
fan

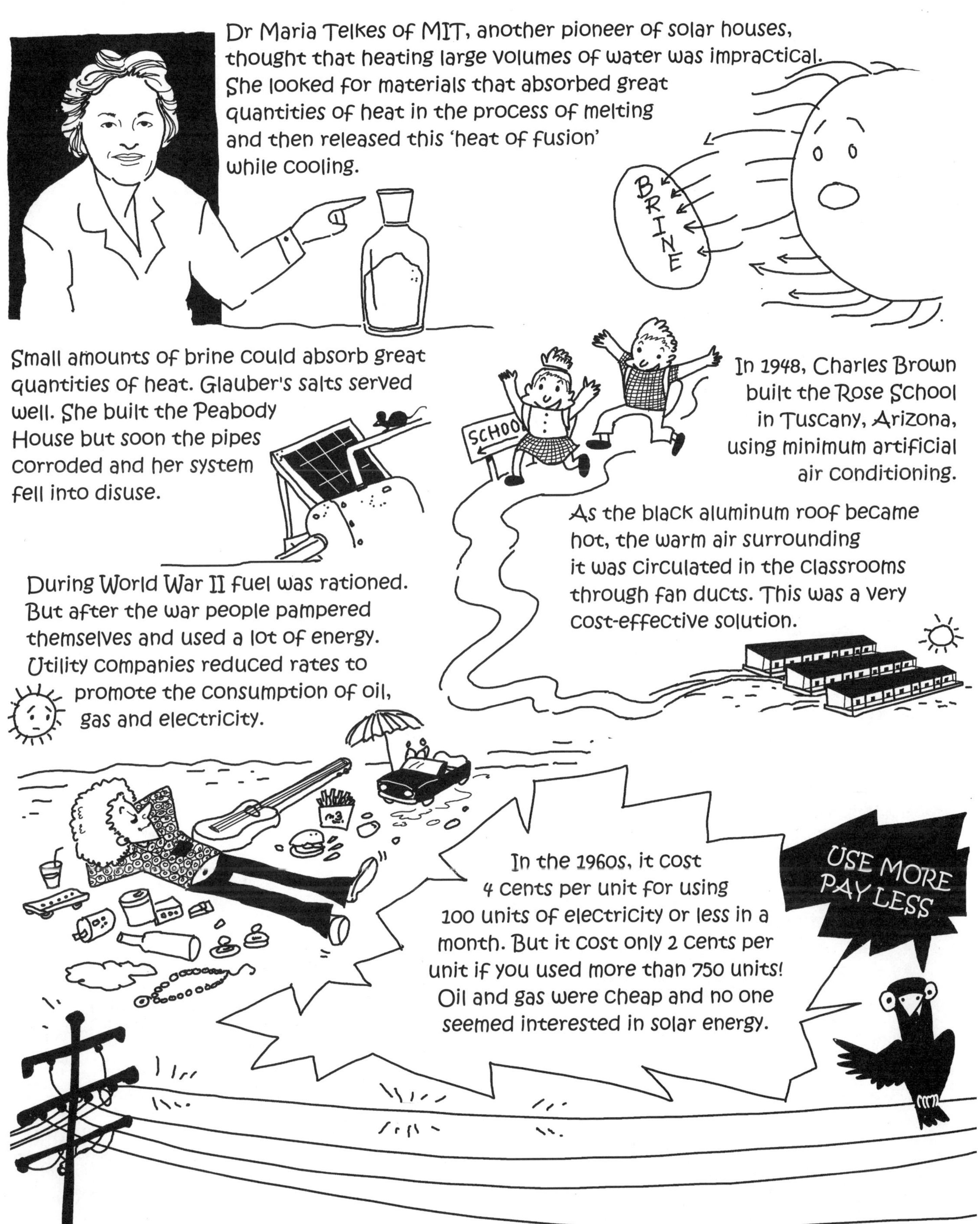
Dr Maria Telkes of MIT, another pioneer of solar houses, thought that heating large volumes of water was impractical. She looked for materials that absorbed great quantities of heat in the process of melting and then released this 'heat of fusion' while cooling.
BRINE
Small amounts of brine could absorb great quantities of heat. Glauber's salts served well. She built the Peabody House but soon the pipes corroded and her system fell into disuse.
SCHOOL
In 1948, Charles Brown built the Rose School in Tuscany, Arizona, using minimum artificial air conditioning.
As the black aluminum roof became hot, the warm air surrounding it was circulated in the classrooms through fan ducts. This was a very cost-effective solution.
During World War II fuel was rationed. But after the war people pampered themselves and used a lot of energy. Utility companies reduced rates to promote the consumption of oil, gas and electricity.
In the 1960s, it cost 4 cents per unit for using 100 units of electricity or less in a month. But it cost only 2 cents per unit if you used more than 750 units! Oil and gas were cheap and no one seemed interested in solar energy.
USE MORE PAY LESS

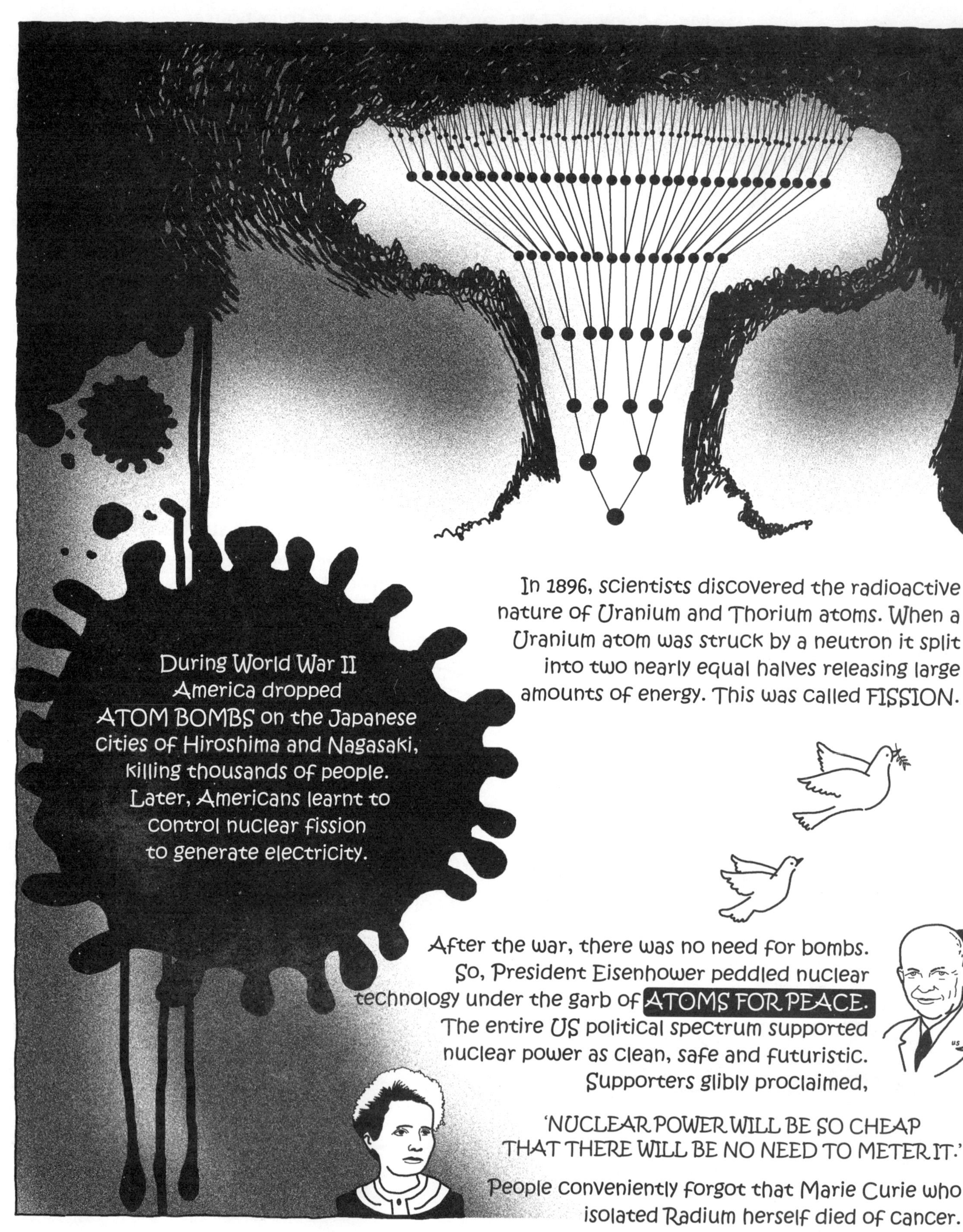
In 1896, scientists discovered the radioactive nature of Uranium and Thorium atoms. When a Uranium atom was struck by a neutron it split into two nearly equal halves releasing large amounts of energy. This was called FISSION.
During World War II America dropped ATOM BOMBS on the Japanese cities of Hiroshima and Nagasaki, killing thousands of people. Later, Americans learnt to control nuclear fission to generate electricity.
After the war, there was no need for bombs. So, President Eisenhower peddled nuclear technology under the garb of ATOMS FOR PEACE. The entire US political spectrum supported nuclear power as clean, safe and futuristic. Supporters glibly proclaimed,
'NUCLEAR POWER WILL BE SO CHEAP THAT THERE WILL BE NO NEED TO METER IT.'
People conveniently forgot that Marie Curie who isolated Radium herself died of cancer.

Nuclear power was the product of war and is still considered unsafe by many. Whether Uranium is mined, or radioactive waste disposed of, radiation contamination is unavoidable. Despite all assurances by the nuclear czars, we have witnessed the Three Mile Island (1979), Chernobyl (1985) and the Fukushima (2011) nuclear disasters. These three accidents caused significant radioactive contamination, endangered the environment and the health of surrounding communities and it will take years to complete the clean-up.

Not a single nuclear power plant has been built in America in the last 40 years. Post Fukushima, Germany has decided to dismantle all existing nuclear plants.

The response to India's 1998 Pokhran nuclear tests was uniformly eulogistic. Politicians across the board lauded this feat. Indian scientists vied for photographs dressed in military fatigues!

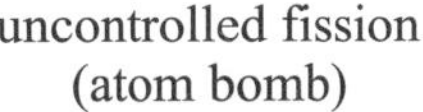

uncontrolled fission (atom bomb)

controlled fission (nuclear energy)

Coal pollutes, it releases carbon dioxide into the atmosphere leading to global warming and change in the earth's climate.

The first lone dissent against nuclear science came from Laurie Baker, a Gandhian architect. He pointed out that Mahatma Gandhi had asked scientists that their work be non-violent, environmentally benign and should help the poor. The atomic test miserably failed all these three criteria of Gandhian science.

Oil is running out. Fierce fighting is on to control the last oil wells in Iraq, Afghanistan and now Libya.

There is an earnest search for alternatives. And it is WIND and SOLAR energy that will hold the fort in the future.

Hydroelectric plants require big dams that displace a lot of people.

SOLAR CELLS

By heating water using sunshine we can cut down only a little on fuel. But if we could convert sunshine directly into electricity it would be a great leap forward.

In 1869, Edmund Becquerel, a French scientist discovered the photovoltaic effect.

Outside the nucleus of the atom spin tiny negatively charged particles called electrons. When some electrons break loose and drift towards other atoms, a current flows.

Sunlight has enough energy to cause the electrons of some atoms to work loose. Such atoms can produce an electric current when exposed to light.

In 1873, when chemist W. Smith shone light on the metal Selenium (an element derived from copper ore), it conducted an electric current. The current was small but soon a use was found for it.

Almost 50 years later Charles Fritts, an American inventor, made the first SOLAR CELLS.

sunlight

photons

electron flow

hole flow

These thin wafers made from Selenium were covered with a transparent gold film. When sunlight struck the cell, 1% of the sun's energy got converted into electricity.

Selenium was used as an ELECTRIC EYE. On sensing light it produced a small current which triggered a relay that allowed a larger current to close a door.

This led to the invention of photometers. They helped in measuring the intensity of light.

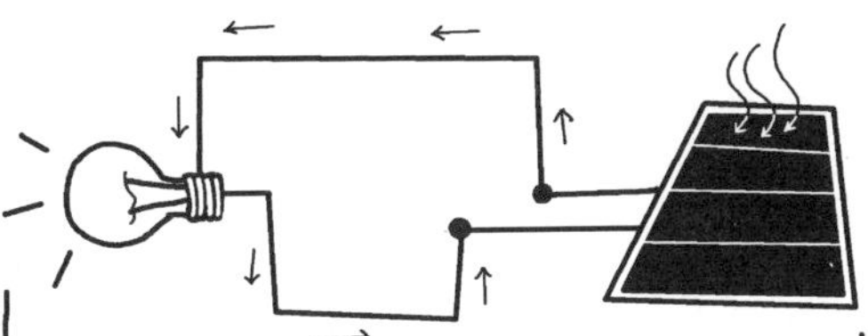

In 1948, semiconductors were discovered. They were made of a pure substance poisoned with a small impurity. Semiconductors ushered in the golden era of transistors.

In 1954, scientists at the Bell Labs made an accidental discovery which revolutionised solar-cell technology. They noticed that when Silicon was exposed to light, an electric current appeared. Silicon converted 5% of the sunlight into electricity. It was much better than Selenium which converted only 1%.

Silicon is abundant in the sand and rocks around us. However, the Silicon-Oxygen bond is very hard to break. Silicon has to be purified and sliced into thin wafers and impregnated with the right impurities. This makes it VERY expensive.

Photovoltaic systems are modular and can be quickly installed. Power can be generated where it is required without the need for transmission lines.
They are reliable and involve no moving parts.
Their operation and maintenance costs are low.

SOLAR WINS SPACE RACE

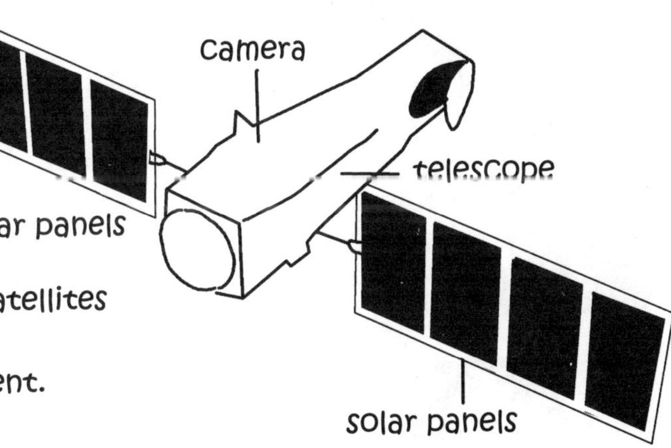

Just as solar cells were being consigned to the curiosity heap the space race came along. Batteries were too heavy to carry in space. As the sun shone 24 hours in outer space, solar cells provided the perfect answer.
Since 1957, solar cells have powered all American satellites from Vanguard to Skylab. Solar cells proved their mettle in space as their high cost was not a deterrent.

However, matters were different on earth. Solar cells couldn't compete. Under pressure from the oil lobby, the American government was not interested in cheap solar cells. Electricity produced by coal, though dirtier, was much cheaper. CO_2 emissions and global warming were still not HOT issues. There was no solar lobby to counter the powerful nuclear juggernaut.

ADVANTAGES OF SOLAR ENERGY

With 300 sunny days in a year, there is great potential in India for harnessing solar energy.

In India, 30% of the electricity generated is lost (or stolen) in transit. Decentralised solar power will reduce these 'losses'.

Solar energy is clean, renewable and sustainable, and will help in protecting our environment. Unlike gas, oil and coal, solar energy does not create any greenhouse gases, global warming, acid rain or smog.

POWER FOR A FEW vs EMPOWERING THE PEOPLE

If every Indian village hut had a solar panel, ordinary people would be empowered.

Improved solar technology can convert almost 20% of the sunlight directly into electricity.

Women in villages often trudge for miles to collect firewood.

Women inhale toxic smoke while cooking on fire and suffer from respiratory diseases.

Solar-cooked food is more nutritious. It preserves more natural elements as the cooking happens at slower and lower temperatures.

You can leave the food to cook on its own without tending it frequently. It is almost impossible to burn food on a solar cooker.

Coal mining leaves the land pock-marked. Oil wells catch fire.
Hydroelectric power entails large-scale displacement of people.
Nuclear power is hazardous right from mining to disposal of radioactive waste.
Solar and wind energy is certainly safer.

Solar energy helps us live in a sustainable manner. It will help us cope better with the uncertainties of disaster, climate change and scarcity.

I've to wait three weeks for the gas cylinder. Kerosene is available only in the black market. But operating a solar cooker is free!

Solar technology will support local jobs and create wealth. It will help boost the local economy.

Solar panels have no moving parts; they are virtually maintenance-free and last for decades. Solar panels may appear more expensive than conventional systems. But large-scale production will cut costs and make this GREEN ENERGY competitive.

As solar energy uses NO fuel, there is no coal, oil or gas to transport over long distances. Unlike nuclear radioactive waste, solar energy produces no waste.

Solar Energy Systems can be installed in remote regions which are far away from power plants. Thousands of houses in Leh, Ladakh have been electrified using solar panels. They are more practical and cost-effective as opposed to conventional grids.

Solar energy does not pollute by releasing carbon dioxide, nitrogen oxide, sulphur dioxide or mercury into the atmosphere.

But many conventional energy systems severely pollute the atmosphere.

Experts have predicted that by 2040, 50% of the world's energy will come from renewable sources.

Currently 2 billion people in the world live in darkness without any electricity.

Solar energy, coupled with low-watt, high-luminosity LED lamps offer an enormous possibility of bringing a ray of hope to the world's poor.

The use of solar energy indirectly reduces health costs.

Where does all the coal, gas and petroleum come from?

The SUN is the source of all non-renewable fossil fuels–coal, oil and gas. All fossil fuels began life as plants or animals. Their energy came from the sun millions of years ago.

Installation of solar water heaters or solar panels helps in reducing electricity bills. They insulate you against frequent powercuts.

The use of solar energy is truly empowering. It reduces dependence on foreign and centralised sources of energy. It can galvanise communities and act as a buffer during natural disasters or international boycotts.

In one hour more sunlight falls on the earth than what is used by the entire population in one year.

Sunlight travels to the earth in approximately 8 minutes from 150 million km away, at 3,00,000 km per second.

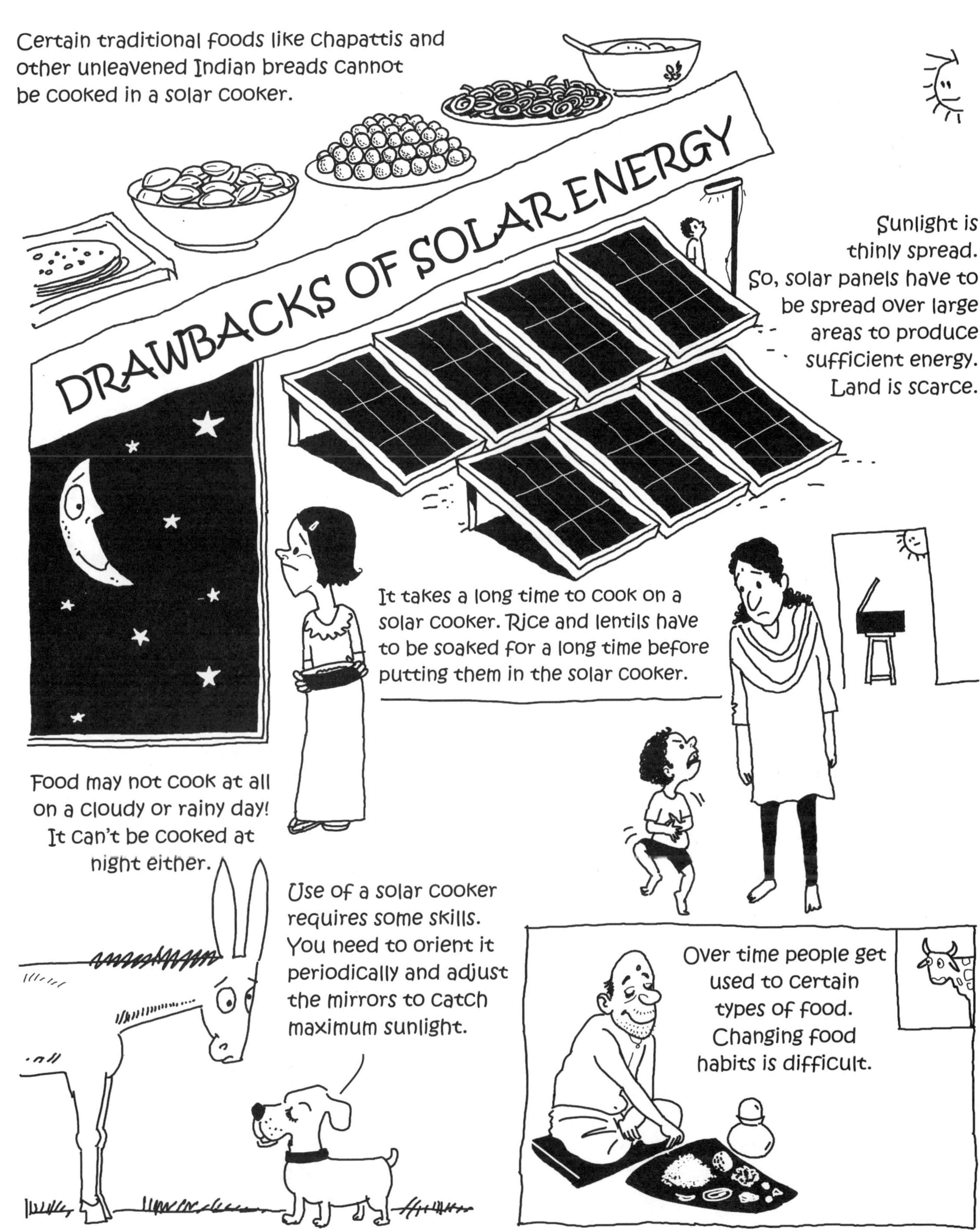
Certain traditional foods like chapattis and other unleavened Indian breads cannot be cooked in a solar cooker.
DRAWBACKS OF SOLAR ENERGY
Sunlight is thinly spread. So, solar panels have to be spread over large areas to produce sufficient energy. Land is scarce.
It takes a long time to cook on a solar cooker. Rice and lentils have to be soaked for a long time before putting them in the solar cooker.
Food may not cook at all on a cloudy or rainy day! It can't be cooked at night either.
Use of a solar cooker requires some skills. You need to orient it periodically and adjust the mirrors to catch maximum sunlight.
Over time people get used to certain types of food. Changing food habits is difficult.

Cooking gas, kerosene, though in short supply are still available at subsidised rates.
As long as fuel (wood, biomass) is available people have little incentive to try out new things.
Both solar cookers and photovoltaic panels have low running costs but high capital costs. Poor people often don't have money to invest. Banks are averse to giving loans to the poor.
Ordinary people are no techno freaks. They are just not used to solar cookers.
● A world record was set in 1990 when a solar-powered aircraft flew 4060 km across the USA, using no fuel.
FACTS ABOUT ENERGY USE
● Electric ovens consume the most electricity, followed by microwave ovens and central air conditioning.
Miss America
● Accounting for only 5% of the world's population, the US consumes 30% of the world's energy.

WORLD EXPERIENCE WITH SOLAR COOKERS

An international aid agency once distributed 500 solar cookers in a refugee colony. After six months they conducted a survey and found that 90% of the solar cookers had been chopped and burnt as firewood!

Solar cookers have been around for a long time. Yet, they have failed to capture the imagination of ordinary people. Why are solar cookers still not popular?

The same question can be asked of other appropriate technologies–smokeless 'chulhas' (cooking ovens), small windmills, micro hydel, etc. This question needs to be probed thoroughly.

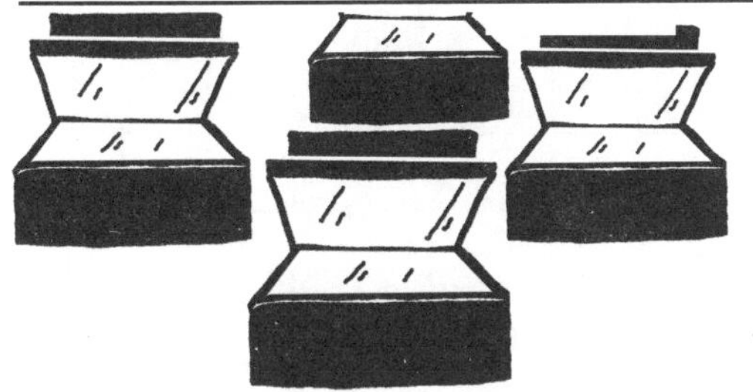

Such experiences enable governments to proclaim:
'SOLAR COOKERS DON'T WORK;
DON'T SUBSIDISE THEM.'

But there are SUCCESS stories too.
Greece gets a lot of sunlight.
In 1980, the Greek government heavily taxed electric geysers and simultaneously provided subsidised, top-quality solar water heaters.
They ran a good publicity campaign.
Solar water heaters caught on.

The Greek MANTRA for success was:

Tax incentives + Good quality + Education + Reasonable price + A simple scheme

We have only scratched the surface. To be truly effective, solar technology needs to be fine-tuned and dovetailed into local cultures. This potential resource can help end world hunger, improve health and mitigate deforestation. Going solar is in the interest of the most underprivileged people of the world.

I want Nuclear

In the 1950s, when Homi Bhabha was setting up atomic reactors in India, skeptics like D. D. Kosambi questioned his wisdom and suggested the use of SOLAR instead of NUCLEAR energy.

TYPES OF SOLAR COOKERS

Box cookers are the commonest solar cookers. Several hundred thousands have been used in India. They are cheap, sturdy, easy to use and can cook many Indian dishes—rice, lentils, vegetables, etc.

Curved concentrator cookers are parabolic in shape. The rays of the sun are collected and concentrated by a large dish on the small black pot hung at the focus. These cookers cook fast at very high temperatures. They are also bigger, more expensive and fit for big institutions.

The simple COOKit is made from cardboard with a shining layer of foil on top. It can be easily folded and stowed away.

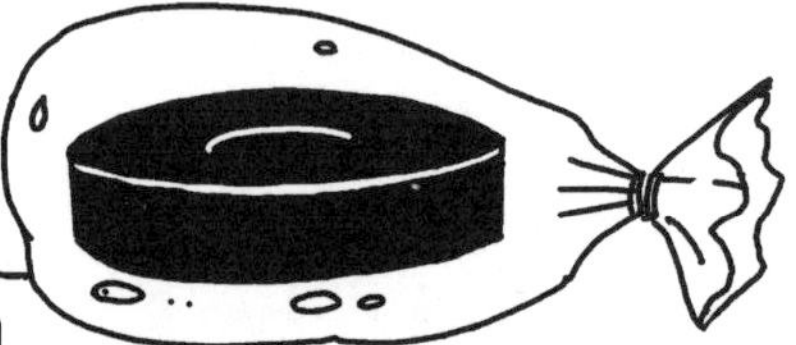

Because it is cheap, the COOKit is widely used. Instead of glass the cooking pot in a COOKit is enclosed in a plastic bag and its mouth is tied.
A transparent heat trap around the dark pot lets in sunlight, but keeps in the heat. This could be a clear transparent heat-resistant plastic bag or the glass covering on top of the box cooker.

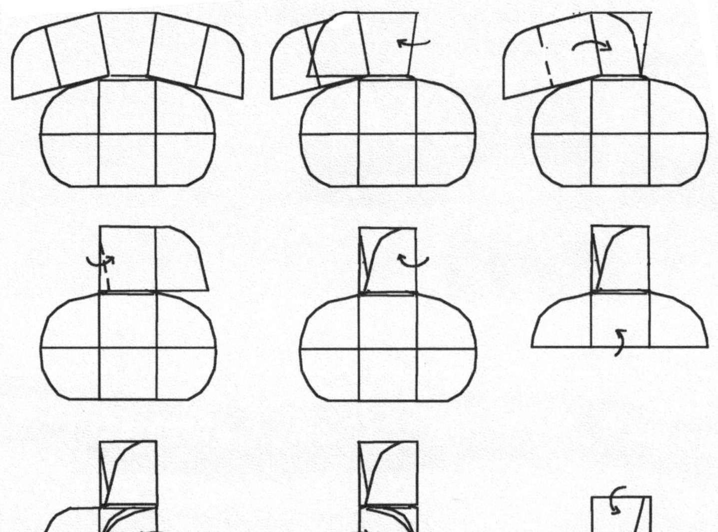

BE ACTIVE TODAY INSTEAD OF BEING RADIOACTIVE TOMORROW!

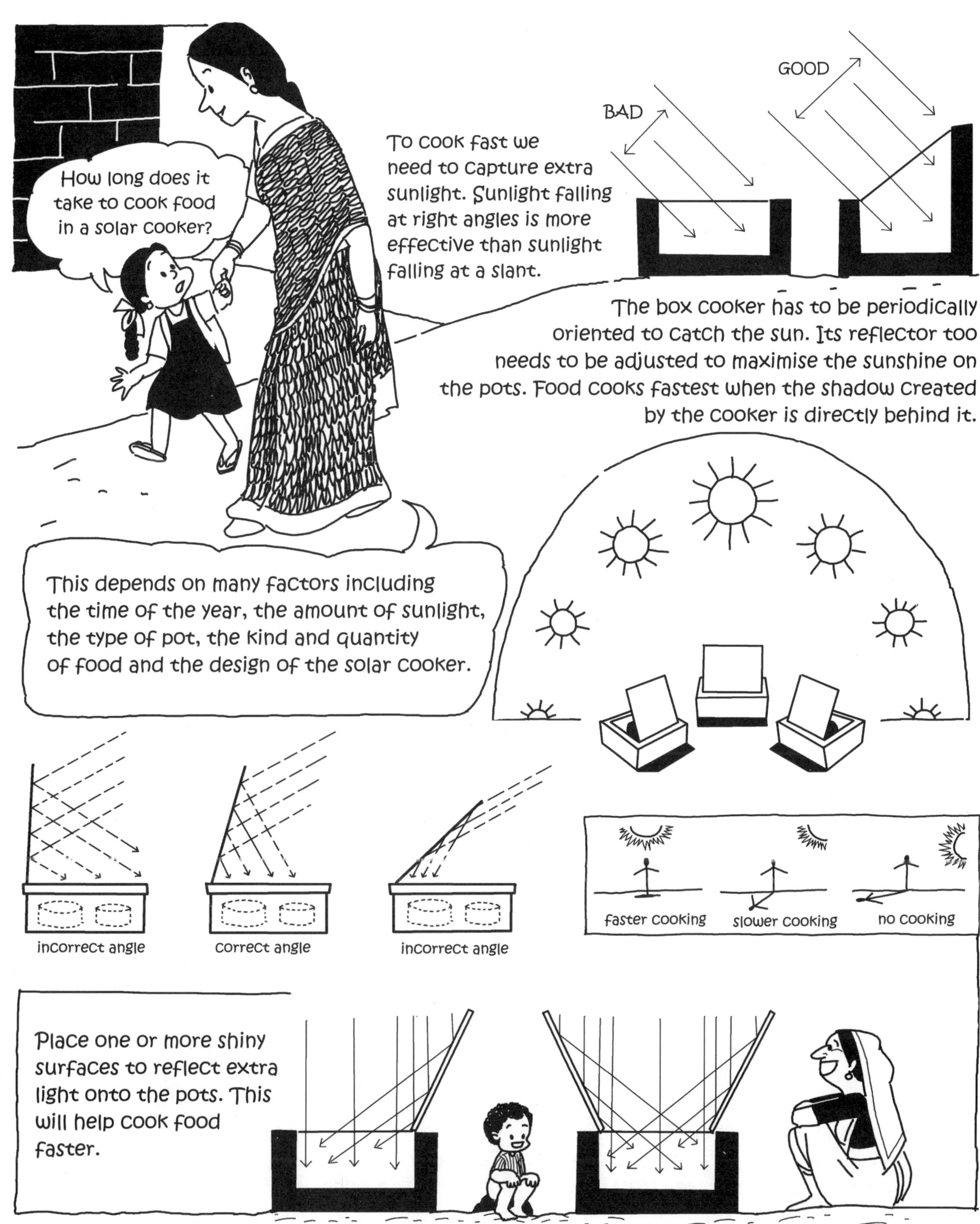
How long does it take to cook food in a solar cooker?
To cook fast we need to capture extra sunlight. Sunlight falling at right angles is more effective than sunlight falling at a slant.
BAD
GOOD
The box cooker has to be periodically oriented to catch the sun. Its reflector too needs to be adjusted to maximise the sunshine on the pots. Food cooks fastest when the shadow created by the cooker is directly behind it.
This depends on many factors including the time of the year, the amount of sunlight, the type of pot, the kind and quantity of food and the design of the solar cooker.
incorrect angle
correct angle
incorrect angle
faster cooking
slower cooking
no cooking
Place one or more shiny surfaces to reflect extra light onto the pots. This will help cook food faster.

CAR TUBE COOKER

This solar cooker was designed by Suresh Vaidyarajan, an architect with a passionate interest in building solar houses.
Here's how you make one:
Take a used car tube and a piece of flat window glass.
Repair a punctured tube and then inflate it.

Place it on a black wooden board.
Place rice + water in a black aluminium cooking pot.
Place the pot in the well and cover the tube with plain glass.

The glass seals the tube so air can't get in or get out.
The inflated tube makes for a good insulated box.
Sun rays enter the glass and get trapped.
Slowly the temperature rises and cooks the rice.

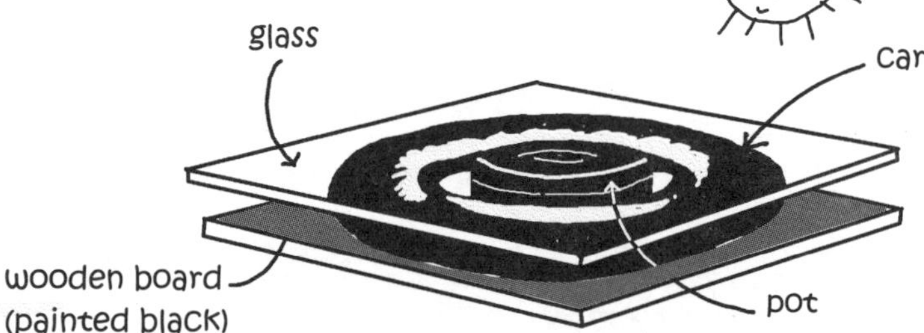

SODIS

A Swedish group has promoted SODIS (Solar Water Disinfection) as a low-cost technique to purify drinking water for the world's underprivileged.

Fill 3/4th of the bottle with water.
Screw the lid and shake well.
The dissolved air in the water helps with disinfection.
Then place the bottle on the roof in the sun.
In a few hours the ultraviolet rays of the sun will destroy all the disease-causing pathogens, and the water will become safe for drinking.
(CHEMICALS can leach out of plastic bottles. So GLASS BOTTLES are SAFER.)

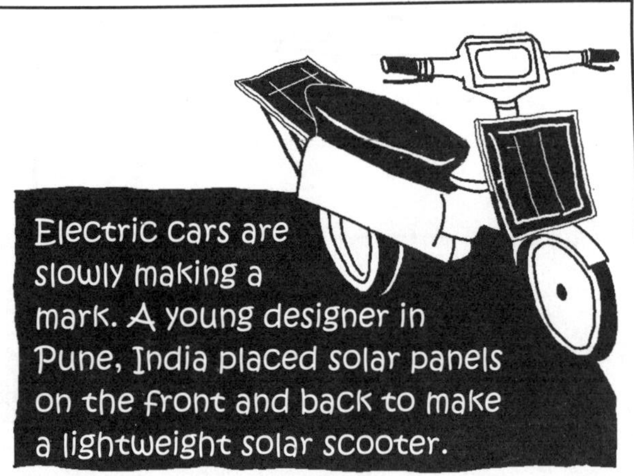

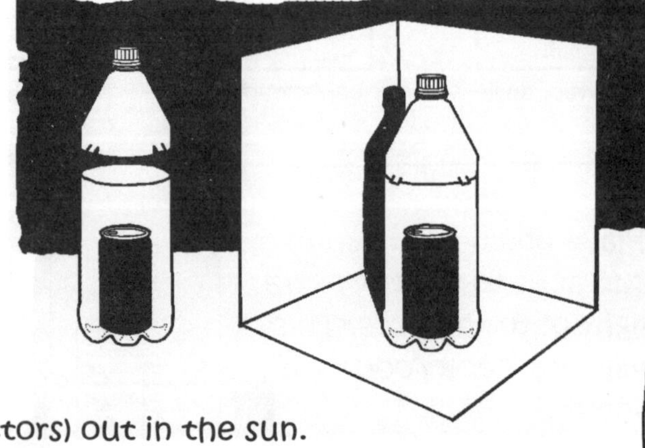

MAKING A SOLAR WATER PURIFIER

Fill a black aluminium can with ordinary tap water. Cut a transparent 2-litre plastic bottle as shown and place the black can in it.
Place the bottle on a shiny surface (with reflectors) out in the sun.
After a few hours in the sun, all the pathogens will be killed and the water will become potable.

Designed by researchers at the M.I.T., this no-cost lighting device has become a craze. A 2-litre plastic bottle filled with water is hung vertically through the roof. A few drops of bleach prevent algal growth. Sunlight enters the bottle from the top. The water disperses sunlight in all directions and the bottle shines like a 60-watt bulb!

LIGHTING HOMES, WINNING HEARTS

Dr Harish Hande, founder of the solar company SELCO in Bangalore, received the 2011 Magsaysay Award for lighting over 1,25,000 rural homes. In the 1980s, Bunker Roy promoted solar energy at the Barefoot College, Tilonia, Rajasthan.

VERY LARGE SOLAR COOKERS

In 1998, the Spiritual World University at Mount Abu set up a large-scale solar cooking system.

Since then it has cooked food for over 20,000 people every day. Similarly, tens of thousands of devotees regularly eat a solar meal at the famous Sai Baba Temple in Shirdi, Maharashtra.

MANY GODS, ONE SUN

Cut out several religious symbols from a narrow strip of cardboard. Go out in the sun and hold the cardboard close to the ground. You'll see the shadows of various signs on the ground. Then, slowly raise the card upwards. The different signs will now all become the same circles. As you lift it higher the circles touch each other, symbolising our essential oneness as human beings and earth citizens. Why does this happen? The circles of light that you see are all images of the sun. They are round because the sun is round.

(Courtesy: Dr. Vivek Monteiro)

'I'd put my money on the sun and solar energy. What a source of power! I hope we don't have to wait till oil and coal run out before we tackle that.' Thomas Edison

BIO-MIMICRY

Every single leaf of a tree is a powerhouse which manufactures food using sunlight. If we could 'bio-mimic' and make solar panels to look like leaves (and make them catch maximum sunlight), imagine how efficient they would be!

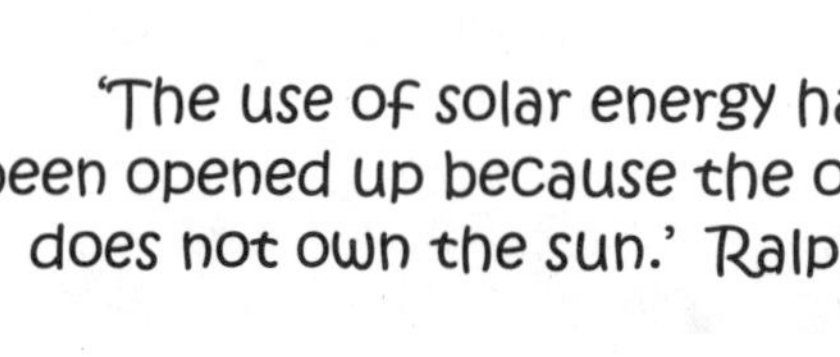

'The use of solar energy has not been opened up because the oil industry does not own the sun.' Ralph Nader

We firmly believe in NUCLEAR POWER.
It has been a reliable source of power in the past.
Hopefully, it will fulfil our future needs too.
However, we don't need numerous nuclear plants.
Just one will do.

It should be really large,
and its power should be available to everyone on earth.

It should have an effective design,
and should last for a long time without modification.

There should be no radioactive waste to deal with,
and it should not be destructible.

Such a NUCLEAR PLANT already exists
150 million kilometers away.
It is our

SUN!

REFERENCES

1. *A Golden Thread 2500 years of Solar Architecture and Technology* Ken Butti and John Perlin
2. *How Did We Find Out About Solar Power?* Isaac Asimov
3. *The Kids Solar Energy Book* Tilly Spetgang, Malcolm Wells
4. *Done in the Sun* Annie Hillerman
5. *Sun Fun* Michael Daley
6. *Ten Little Fingers* Arvind Gupta
7. *Solar Cookers International* http://www.solarcooking.org/
8. *An Abbreviated History of Fossil Fuels* Post Carbon Institute
9. *Solar Energy - An Awakening* a film by Dr Govind Kulkarni
10. *Sun or Atom* D. D. Kosambi
11. *Solar Energy for the Underdeveloped Countries* D. D. Kosambi
12. *The Last Quaker in India* Ramachandra Guha